P9-BTN-102

FRANKLIN PIERCE
COLLEGE LIBRARY
RINDGE, N.H. 03461

Holiday Magic Books

Arbor Day
MAGIC

by James W. Baker
pictures by George Overlie

Lerner Publications Company Minneapolis

CURR
GT
5150
.B327
A7
1990

To my fellow magicians in the Philippines, especially members of the Philippine Amateur League of Magicians (PALM), for giving me the honor of serving as PALM's first president during my tour of duty in Manila.

Copyright © 1990 by Lerner Publications Company

All rights reserved. International copyright secured.
No part of this book may be reproduced in any form whatsoever
without permission in writing from the publisher except for the
inclusion of brief quotations in an acknowledged review.

Library of Congress Cataloging-in-Publication Data
Baker, James W. 1926-
    Arbor Day magic/by James W. Baker; pictures by George Overlie.
       p.   cm.—(Holiday magic books)
    Summary: Explains how to perform magic tricks revolving around an
Arbor Day theme.
    ISBN 0-8225-2235-7
    1. Tricks—Juvenile literature. 2. Arbor Day—Juvenile
literature.   [1. Magic tricks. 2. Arbor Day.] I. Overlie,
George, ill. II. Title. III. Series: Baker, James W., 1926-
Holiday magic books.
GV1548.B327 1990
793.8—dc20
                                                89-37229
                                                   CIP
                                                    AC

Manufactured in the United States of America

1 2 3 4 5 6 7 8 9 10 99 98 97 96 95 94 93 92 91 90

CONTENTS

INTRODUCTION

Johnny Appleseed roamed the American frontier in the early 1800s, planting trees and giving apple seeds to the people he met. He wanted to make sure there would be plenty of trees for years to come.

On Arbor Day, you can be like Johnny Appleseed. You can plant a tree yourself and remind others of the value of trees by having an Arbor Day magic show. Just "leaf" through these pages and learn some Arbor Day tricks. Then you can plant the seeds of magic among your friends!

DRAWING A TREE

HOW IT LOOKS

Put four large index cards, each with a picture of a different kind of tree on it, out on a table for the audience to see. One tree is filled with leaves, one has bare branches, one is a fir tree, and one tree is chopped down. Your assistant is in another room with the door closed. A volunteer from the audience chooses one of the drawings and holds it up for the rest of the audience to see. A pad of paper is sent out to your assistant, who draws a duplicate of the selected tree on the pad even though she hasn't even been in the room.

8

1. You will need four large index cards. On each one, draw a picture of a different kind of tree (**Figure 1**).

figure 1.

2. You will also need a pad of paper, a piece of cardboard slightly bigger than the pad, and a bulldog clip. Your assistant will need a pencil or pen.

1. Tell the audience that your assistant is in another room with the door closed. Point out the four pictures and have a volunteer choose one and hold it up for the rest of the audience to see.

2. Hand another volunteer the piece of cardboard with a pad of paper on it, held in place by the bulldog clip, and ask him to take this to your assistant in the other room.

3. As you pick up the cardboard with the pad of paper on it, you must make a slight adjustment of the pad to signal to your assistant which picture was selected. The code is as follows:

A. A wide margin on the right indicates the leafy tree was selected.

B. A wide margin on the left shows the bare tree was chosen.

C. Equal margins show the fir tree was selected.

D. A wide margin at top means the chopped-down tree is the chosen one (**Figure 2**).

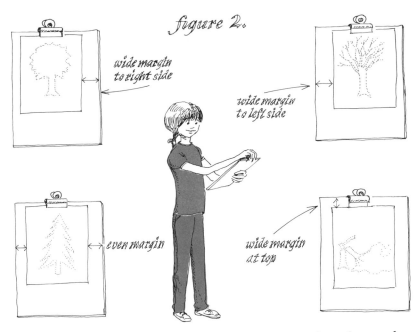

figure 2.

wide margin to right side

wide margin to left side

even margin

wide margin at top

4. You and your assistant must memorize the code ahead of time, of course. When your assistant looks at the arrangement of the pad of paper on the cardboard, she knows precisely which tree to draw.

THAT BLOOMING TREE

HOW IT LOOKS

Show the audience a picture of a cherry tree in winter. It has no leaves or fruit, only bare branches. Fold the picture, put it in a canning jar, and screw on the top of the jar. Say something like, "as the months passed, along came snow, wind, rain, and sunshine," as you show a picture of each. Unscrew the lid and take the picture out of the jar. The tree has a full set of leaves and there's even a cherry in the jar.

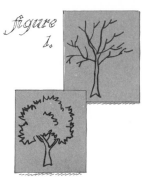

figure 1.

1. On one piece of construction paper, draw a tree with bare branches. On a second piece of construction paper, the same size and color as the first, draw a tree with leaves (**Figure 1**).

2. On separate sheets of paper, draw pictures of snow, wind, rain, and sunshine (**Figure 2**).

figure 2.

3. You will need a real cherry.

4. You will also need the kind of canning jar with the quilted crystal pattern on it. The pattern will slightly distort the contents of the jar.

figure 3.

cardboard insert covered with foil

canning jar with quilted crystal pattern

fold picture of leafy tree and put it and the cherry in the back half of the jar

figure 4.

5. Cut a piece of cardboard so that it can divide the inside of the jar in half (**Figure 3**). Cover the cardboard with aluminum foil. Stick a tiny piece of clear tape on the back of the jar so you will be able to feel the difference between the front and the back.

6. Put the folded picture of the leafy tree and the cherry in the back half of the jar, behind the foil-covered insert (**Figure 4**). Because of the insert, the tree and cherry will be invisible to the audience and the jar will appear empty.

1. Show the audience the picture of the bare tree. Fold the picture and put it in front of the insert. Be sure to fold this picture exactly the way you folded the hidden picture of the tree with leaves. Screw the lid on the jar.

2. As you talk about the months passing, show the pictures of snow, wind, rain, and sunshine, holding each one in front of the jar.

3. As you hold up the sunshine with one hand, use your other hand to twist the jar 180 degrees— touching the tape to know how far to turn the jar. The leafy tree and the cherry are now in front.

4. Unscrew the lid and take the folded picture of the leafy tree out of the jar. Unfold the picture and show that the tree now has a full set of leaves. Then take out the cherry. The other tree—the bare one—will be safely hidden behind the foil-covered insert which makes the jar appear to be empty.

THE LAST TREE LOSES

HOW IT LOOKS

Challenge your friend to a game of "the last tree loses." Fifteen slips of paper, each bearing the name of a different tree, are on the table. You and your friend take turns picking up trees. A player may pick up one, two, or three trees — but no more — on each turn. The object is to avoid being the player who picks up the last tree on the table because the one who does that is the loser. You win every time because you know the secret.

Cut 15 little pieces of paper, each about 2 inches (5 cm) square, out of different colors of construction paper. Write the name of a different tree on each square (**Figure 1**). Lay the squares on the table with the names of the trees faceup.

apple
hickory
oak
birch
magnolia
holly
locust
pine
willow
palm
aspen
cottonwood
maple
elm
redbud

figure 1.

1. Explain the rules to your friend: each player takes turns picking up trees. A player may pick up one, two, or three trees—but no more—on each turn. The player who picks up the last tree on the table is the loser.

2. From the beginning, you keep track of the total number of trees that have been picked up by both players.

3. Make sure you pick up the 10th tree. If you do, you can't lose. Here's why:

  A. When you take the 10th tree there will be five trees left on the table and it will be your friend's turn.

  B. If he takes one tree, you take three, leaving him with the last one on the table.

  C. If he takes two trees, you take two, leaving him again with the last tree on the table.

  D. If he takes three trees, you take one, leaving him with the last tree on the table.

THE STUBBORN OAK

HOW IT LOOKS

Tell the audience a story that goes something like, "In a forest grew an oak that was so stubborn that it refused to be cut. Every time a lumberjack came into the forest to cut the oak down, it refused to remain cut and magically restored itself." Say that you would like to illustrate the story but because you don't have a tree handy, you will use the next best thing—a piece of newspaper, since paper is made from trees. Fold the paper and cut it with a pair of scissors. But when you unfold it, it is still in one piece. Repeat this several times to show how stubborn the oak was.

1. For this trick, you will need a sheet of newspaper, rubber cement, and a pair of scissors. You will also need talcum powder, flour, or cornstarch.

2. Secretly prepare the paper as follows:

figure 1.

30"

|← 2" →|

figure 2.

   A. Cut a strip of newspaper about 2 inches (5 cm) wide and about 30 inches (75 cm) long (**Figure 1**).

   B. Crease the strip in half (**Figure 2**).

C. Apply rubber cement to an area of the strip about 4 inches (10 cm) above and 4 inches (10 cm) below the crease (**Figure 3**).

D. Spread the rubber cement evenly and allow it to dry. Repeat this twice, allowing the rubber cement to dry between applications.

E. Now sprinkle talcum powder, flour or corn starch over the rubber cemented area, spread it around, and shake off the excess powder.

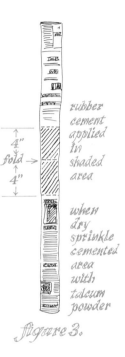

rubber cement applied in shaded area

when dry sprinkle cemented area with talcum powder

figure 3.

HOW TO DO IT

1. As you tell the story from the section on HOW IT LOOKS, show the audience the newspaper strip unfolded, and then fold it in half.

21

2. With the scissors, cut through both halves of the strip, about ½ inch (1 cm) from the fold (**Figure 4**). The cut-off piece will flutter to the floor.

3. Pick up one end of the paper strip and let the other end fall. The paper strip looks like it is still in one piece. It has actually been cut, but a thin film of rubber cement—pressed together by the scissors when you cut through the paper—holds the two pieces together.

4. You can repeat the cuts a few more times. Each time the paper appears to have restored itself. You can do this as long as you cut in the area where you applied the rubber cement.

5. Conclude the trick by telling your audience that the stubborn tree just refused to be cut down.

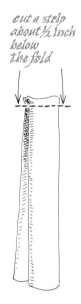

cut a strip about ½ inch below the fold

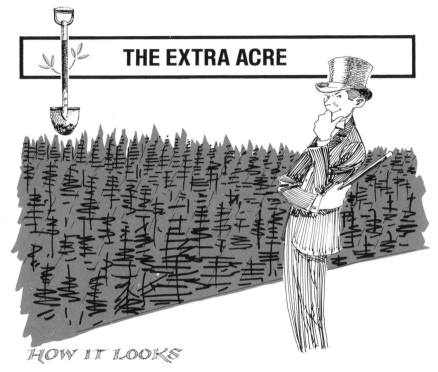

THE EXTRA ACRE

HOW IT LOOKS

Tell your friend a story about a magician who had a tree farm that was 64 acres square. He wanted to plant more trees, so by magic he discovered a way to add an extra acre to his land.

23

1. For this trick, you will need a square piece of cardboard, 8 x 8 inches.
2. Draw lines on the cardboard square exactly as shown (**Figure 1**) and cut along these lines. Note that the pieces are lettered A, B, C, and D.
3. You will also need a ruler.

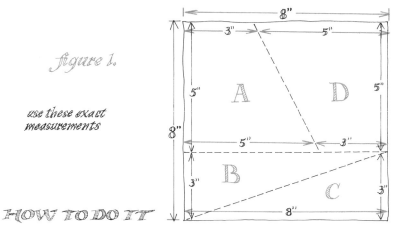

figure 1.

use these exact measurements

1. Tell your friend about the magician who had a tree farm that was 64 acres square.

2. Show the cardboard with the pieces pushed together to form a square (**Figure 1**).

3. Measure the square and show your friend that it is exactly 8 x 8 inches or 64 square inches (8 x 8 = 64). Tell your friend that inches represent acres in this story. Tell how the magician wanted to get an extra acre for planting trees.

4. Showing what the magician did, rearrange the four pieces of cardboard as shown (**Figure 2**).

5. Now measure the cardboard. It is 13 x 5 inches. And 13 x 5 = 65. Using the same land (cardboard), the magician has gained an extra acre of land.

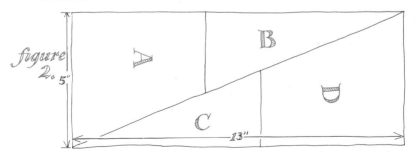

figure 2.

5"

13"

A   B   C   D

GIFTS FROM TREES

HOW IT LOOKS

Hand out five index cards to five members of the audience and ask each person to write the name of something that trees provide. Have a volunteer from the audience collect the five cards, place them facedown on a table, and mix them up. You name each card without looking at it, then pick up that card as you name the next card. After you have named all five cards, turn them over so the audience can read them. They see you were correct every time.

1. For this trick, you will need a few pencils and a stack of five index cards, one of which has a slightly bent corner that will not be noticed by the audience.

2. You will also need a "stooge"—a friend in the audience to help you with the trick. The audience will not know about the stooge.

corner
slightly bent →
RUBBER SHADE NUTS SYRUP NESTS

HOW TO DO IT

1. Hand five index cards to five members of the audience and ask them to write down the name of something that trees provide. Make sure your stooge gets the card marked with the bent corner.

If the audience needs help thinking of things that trees provide, you might mention: lumber, paper, fruits, nuts, olives, syrup, rubber, turpentine, nests, baskets, flowers, medicines, shade, erosion and weather control, fuel, oxygen, and mulch.

2. You and the stooge have agreed ahead of time what he will write on his card, for example, "rubber."

3. Have a volunteer collect all the cards, place them facedown on the table, and mix them up. Even though they're mixed up, you will be able to spot the "rubber" because of the bent corner.

4. You say something like, "I believe this is 'rubber.'" Then pick up any card *other than* the one which really has "rubber" written on it. Look at the face of that card and smile with satisfaction as if you are correct.

5. Read the card you just picked up, for example, the first card says "fruit." Pretend to concentrate and say, "I believe the next card is 'fruit.'" Pick up the next card, look at it, and again smile as if you're correct.

6. Continue to do this with all the cards, saying, "I believe the next card is..." and naming what is written on the card you just picked up.

7. When you have named four facedown cards say, "I believe the next card is..." and name the one you have just picked up, but pick up the last card—the one with the bent corner.

8. Place the "rubber" card at the *beginning* of the stack of cards in your hand, as if it were the *first* card you picked up.

9. Show the cards to your audience. They will be the cards in the order you named even though you did not know what people would write and the cards were facedown and mixed up on the table.

THE CHOSEN TREE

The names of 10 different trees are written in large letters on large index cards folded like pup tents and placed at various points around a room. You go out of the room while someone in the room touches one of the cards. Return to the room and your assistant points to the cards one by one. You are magically able to tell which one was chosen while you were out of the room.

1. For this trick, you will need 10 large index cards. Fold them over like pup tents and, with a magic marker, print the name of a different tree on each one (**Figure 1**).

2. You will also need an assistant who knows the secret to the trick.

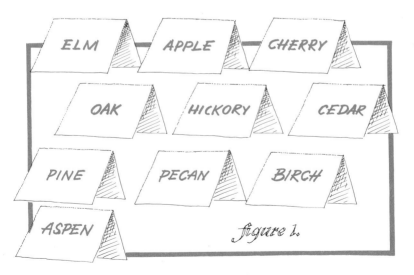

figure 1.

31

Usually, in tricks like this, the assistant gives a signal to the magician. But in this case, the magician signals the assistant.

1. After you return to the room, rest one of your hands on a chair while your assistant points to various tree cards.

2. When you *remove* your hand from the chair, your assistant *then* points to the chosen tree.

3. If you repeat the trick, you lean against the wall as your assistant points to different trees.

4. When you walk away from the wall, your assistant points to the chosen tree.

signal by removing hand from chair

signal by walking away from the wall

THE KNOTTY PINE

HOW IT LOOKS

Tell the audience a story that goes something like, "Many years ago, when a pine tree was very young and easily bent, someone tied a knot in it." You tie a knot in a large, silky scarf. Continue with, "The pine grew up to be a large tree, but its trunk was still tied in a knot—and the pine was very unhappy about this. A magician came into the woods and discovered the unhappy pine, wiggled his fingers, and made the knot untie itself." As you say this, the knot in the scarf mysteriously unties itself.

33

1. You will need a large, dark, silky scarf, about 3 feet (1 m) square, and a thin, black thread, about 3 feet (1 m) long.

2. Tie one end of the black thread to one corner of the scarf. At the other end of the thread, tie several knots, one on top of the other, to form a little thread ball (**Figure 1**).

3. To perform this trick, you must be standing about 10 feet (3 m) back from the audience and wearing dark pants. Also, the room should not be too bright.

dark pants

figure 1.

black thread three feet long

knot

1. As you tell the story from the section on HOW IT LOOKS, hold the scarf with your left hand. Hold it by the corner opposite from the corner where the thread is tied. The thread will hang down, with some of it on the floor.

2. When you tell about the knot being tied in the pine tree, tie a knot in the scarf. Ignore the thread. Let it follow along as you tie the knot in the scarf.

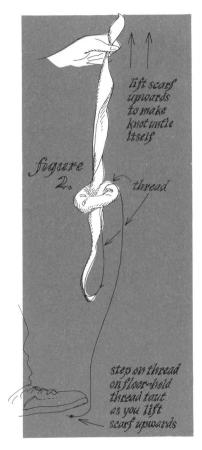

lift scarf upwards to make knot untie itself

figure 2.

thread

step on thread on floor—hold thread taut as you lift scarf upwards

35

3. Continue to hold the knotted scarf in your left hand as you tell about the magician coming into the woods. Step on the end of the thread on the floor (**Figure 2**). The knotted ball will help you hold the thread tight on the floor.

4. When you tell about the magician wiggling his fingers, wiggle your right fingers and gently lift up the scarf with your left hand, keeping your foot on the knotted thread.

5. The thread, unnoticed by the audience, will cause the knot in the scarf to untie itself in a most mysterious manner.

WACKY TREE CARD

Show the audience a piece of construction paper with a single tree drawn on it. Turn the paper over and show the other side; there are four trees. Turn the piece of paper over again and the audience sees three trees instead of one. Once again, turn the paper over and the audience sees six trees. Turn the paper over one last time and show the audience that it is covered with trees.

HOW TO MAKE IT

1. For this trick, you will need two pieces of light-colored construction paper, each 5 x 7 inches (13 x 18 cm), and a dark crayon.

2. Crease one of the pieces of construction paper in half across the center and paste half of that piece of paper to the other piece to make a card (**Figure 1**).

3. With the top half of the paper folded down, draw 10 to 15 trees on the card (**Figure 2**).

4. Fold the flap up and draw two trees on the card as shown (**Figure 3**).

5. Flip the entire card over and draw five trees on the other side as shown (**Figure 4**).

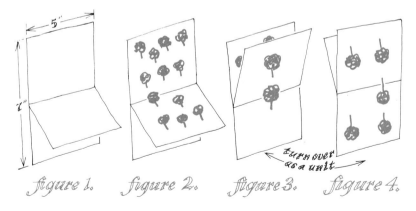

figure 1.   figure 2.   figure 3.   figure 4.

You need to make the audience think you have just a single piece of paper—not two pieces pasted together—so don't let them see the flap while performing the trick.

1. Begin with the flap closed. With your right hand, hold the card with two trees on it toward the audience. Cover the tree near the edge of the card with your four fingers so that the audience sees only one tree (**Figure 5**). Your thumb will be on the back of the card.

figure 5.

2. With your left hand, reach up behind the card, cover the middle tree with your four fingers, and turn the card over. The audience sees four trees (**Figure 6**).

3. With your right hand, reach behind the card and cover the blank spot with your four fingers on the side of the card facing you. Turn the card over, saying there are three trees on this side. The audience will think that there are three trees and your fingers are covering one tree (**Figure 7**).

figure 6.

figure 7.

4. With your left hand, reach up behind the card and cover the blank spot with your fingers. Turn the card over, saying there are six trees on this side. The audience will think that there are six trees and your fingers are covering one of the trees (**Figure 8**).

figure 8.

figure 9.

5. With your right thumb, lift the flap—facing you, not the audience—up and hold it tight. You will be looking at numerous trees. Turn the entire card over and show the audience that it is literally covered with trees (**Figure 9**).

PREDICTING A TREE

HOW IT LOOKS

Write a prediction on a slip of paper, fold it up and place it in plain view, without letting your friend see what you have written. Then ask your friend to write down any number between 50 and 100 and do some math. Show your friend a long list of trees and ask her to count down to the tree at the number arrived at in her math. She will then see that you correctly predicted the tree ahead of time even though you did not know which number she would originally choose.

For this trick, you will need two slips of paper, a pencil, and a list of trees (**Figure 1**).

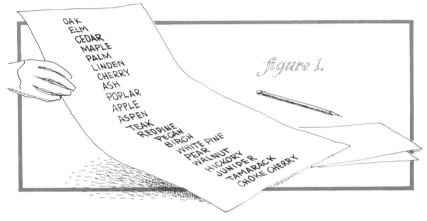

OAK
ELM
CEDAR
MAPLE
PALM
LINDEN
CHERRY
ASH
POPLAR
APPLE
ASPEN
TEAK
REDPINE
PECAN
BIRCH
WHITE PINE
PEAR
WALNUT
HICKORY
JUNIPER
TAMARACK
CHOKE CHERRY

figure 1.

1. Show the list of trees to your friend.
2. Write a prediction—the name of the 12th tree on the list—on a slip of paper, fold it up, and place it in plain view without letting your friend know what you have written.

3. Ask your friend to write down any number between 50 and 100. Tell her to add 82 to the selected number. Then cross out the first digit in her answer and add it to the two-digit number remaining. Then subtract her second answer from her original number. Then add 5 to her third answer. Finally, tell her to subtract 10 from her fourth answer to arrive at her lucky number.

For example:

Choose any number between 50 and 100 . . .   72

Add 82 . . . . + 82

Cross out the first digit in her answer X54

Add that digit to her remaining answer . . . . + 1

To get her second answer   55

Subtract her second answer from her original number	72 − 55
To get her third answer	17
Add 5	+ 5
To get her fourth answer	22
Subtract 10	− 10
To arrive at her lucky number	12

4. Ask your friend to count down from the top to the tree which is listed at her lucky number. Have her look at the tree you predicted earlier. Your prediction is correct.

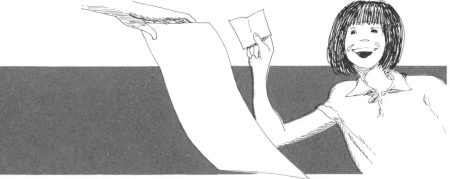

TRICKS FOR BETTER MAGIC

Here are some simple rules you should keep in mind while learning to perform the tricks in this book.

1. Read the entire trick several times until you thoroughly understand it.
2. Practice the trick alone or in front of a mirror until you feel comfortable doing the trick, then present it to an audience.
3. Learn to perform one trick perfectly before moving on to another trick. It is better to perform one trick well than a half dozen poorly.
4. Work on your "presentation." Make up special "patter" (what you say while doing a trick) that is funny and entertaining. Even the simplest trick becomes magical when it is properly presented.
5. Choose tricks that suit you and your personality. Some tricks will work better for you than others.

Stick with these. *Every* trick is not meant to be performed by *every* magician.

6. Feel free to experiment and change a trick to suit you and your unique personality so that you are more comfortable presenting it.

7. Never reveal the secret of the trick. Your audience will respect you much more if you do not explain the trick. When asked how you did a trick, simply say "by magic."

8. Never repeat a trick for the same audience. If you do, you will have lost the element of surprise and your audience will probably figure out how you did it the second time around.

9. Take your magic seriously, but not yourself. Have fun with magic and your audience will have fun along with you.

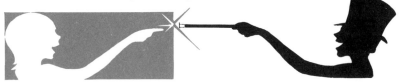

ABOUT THE AUTHOR

James W. Baker, a magician for over 30 years, has performed as "Mister Mystic" in hospitals, orphanages, and schools around the world. He is a member of the International Brotherhood of Magicians and the Society of American Magicians, and is author of *Illusions Illustrated*, a magic book for young performers.

From 1951 to 1963, Baker was a reporter for *The Richmond (VA) News Leader*. From 1963 to 1983, he was an editor with the U.S. Information Agency, living in Washington, D.C., India, Turkey, Pakistan, the Philippines, and Tunisia, and traveling in 50 other countries. Today Baker and his wife, Elaine, live in Williamsburg, Virginia, where he performs magic and writes for the local newspaper, *The Virginia Gazette*.

ABOUT THE ARTIST

George Overlie is a talented artist who has illustrated numerous books. Born in the small town of Rose Creek, Minnesota, Overlie graduated from the New York Phoenix School of Design and began his career as a layout artist. He soon turned to book illustration and proved his skill and versatility in this demanding field. For Overlie, fantasy, illusion, and magic are all facets of illustration and have made doing the Holiday Magic books a real delight.